Orchids of Telangana State:

A Field Guide for Identification

Sitaram Prasad Panda
Yasaswinee Rout
Peddi Harikrishna

Qurate
quratebooks.com

ORCHIDS OF TELANGANA STATE: A Field Guide for Identification
Sitaram Prasad Panda, Yasaswinee Rout & Peddi Harikrishna

Published in 2025

© Published by

Qurate
qaratebooks.com

Qurate Books Pvt. Ltd.
Goa 403523, India
www.quratebooks.com
Tel: 1800-210-6527, Email: info@quratebooks.com

ISBN: 978-93-58983-54-8

Contents

Preface

Orchidaceae, number of species wise is the largest family of flowering plants in India. On the basis of its population they are however one of the least occurring groups of plants. It is because they are restricted to a few geographical areas, mainly due to the aerial mode of living of most (73%) of its members. In India, and especially in Telangana it has not been introduced into the garden noticeably and therefore, most of the plant lovers are not well acquainted with it. The difficulty in maintenance of orchid plants in house and garden also deter many to grow orchid.

The presence of orchids in a forest habitat signifies that it is a healthy forest. Orchids thus serve as an indicator species and deserve special attention. Because of poor germination mechanism the regeneration of orchids is scarce in the wild. Although an herb, they are slow growing plants. It takes a plant about 6-8 years from germination to flowering. They are dwindling quite fast from the wild due to shrinkage of their habitat. Macro-climatic changes have also contributing adversely to the growth and regeneration of orchids. Over-collection of orchids from the wild is another cause of their disappearance from natural habitat. Often nursery man, an enthusiastic plant lover takes out orchid from the wild not knowing its endangered status and conservation value. Even students of plant science commit the same mistake. In almost all the cases such plants face lingering death in the custody of the plant collector. Orchid should not therefore be allowed to be collected indiscriminately from the wild. They have been placed under the restricted group of plants in the Wild life (Protection) Act 1972. Habitats of orchid need to be protected for saving this wonderful group of plants of heritage value.

As a very colourful member of forest habitat, orchids however do not get any special attention in the management of forest or even in the protected habitat; mainly due to lack of knowledge of field staff to identify and its propagation technique. Their exact location and growth status has not been documented due to paucity of authentic data. This field guide aims to provide a hands-on-tool for the foresters, researchers and plant lovers to identify wild orchids by observing some of its basic features.

Authors

Acknowledgements

We extend our sincere gratitude to Dr. A.A. Mao, Director of the Botanical Survey of India (BSI) in Kolkata, for generously providing the essential facilities. The authors are also grateful to Dr. L. Rasingam, Scientist-E & Head of Office, BSI, DRC, Hyderabad for his suggestions and help in various ways. We are very much thankful to Dr. Sarat Misra, Retd. Chief Engineer and Orchidologist, Bhubaneswar, Odisha for his kind help and support. Indebted thanks are due to Dr. C. Sathish Kumar, Retired Scientist, JNTBGRI and Renowned Orchidologist, Thiruvanathpuram, Kerala for providing some orchid photographs along with kind permission to use them. We are further indebted to Dr. S. S. Dash, Scientist-F and In-Charge of the Technical Section, for his unwavering support. Finally, we wish to express our thanks to Dr. P. C. Panda, Retd. Principal Scientist, Regional Plant Resource Centre (RPRC), Bhubaneswar, Odisha and Dr. Jewan Singh Jalal, Scientist-E, BSI Headquarters, Kolkata for providing few photographs.

We are thankful for the helps provided by the Telangana Forest Department. The Financial Supports of the MoEF & CC, Government of India, New Delhi is duly acknowledged.

Authors

Introduction

From all over the world, plant life has an amazing variety of shapes, each specifically adapted to the unique geographic and climatic features of its home. Of these varied botanical treasures, the family Orchidaceae, including the enchanting orchids, has developed an extraordinary worldwide distribution, thriving in virtually every habitat except most inhospitable hot and cold deserts. Among India's luxuriant and diversified flora, Orchidaceae is a uniquely prevalent family of the monocots.

In order to survive in this wide range of environments, orchids have developed remarkable vegetative adaptations to ensure survival and maximize the process of obtaining vital resources. These herbs are perennial, with a high degree of adaptability, being terrestrial plants they can produce their own foods (autotrophs), saprophytes that feed on rotting organic matter, or epiphytes, growing over host plants on the branches and trunks of trees. These epiphytes, having specialized organs to store food and water, are more highly adapted than their non-epiphytic relatives.

Orchids are most renowned, perhaps, for the stunningly diverse and incredibly gorgeous flowers. The flowers offer a range of shape, color, and delicate ornamentation that is unmatched, commonly resembling different life forms with unsettling accuracy, for example, butterflies, bees, scorpions, lizards, snakes, and even human beings or ghostly apparitions. In addition, orchids hybridize with ease, both within and across genera, creating inter specific and intergeneric hybrids that are often more beautiful than the parent plants. Orchid flowers of many species have a long flowering period, with those having a thick, waxy character having excellent vase-life serving excellently in floriculture industries world over.

Orchidaceae's success as a plant family is surely attributable to the evolutionary benefits of the epiphytic habit. This means of living is a testament to the orchids' incredible survival mechanisms. These highly complex plants have fascinated botanists, but their fascinations have long been greater than an academic interest. Orchids are something precious in the hearts of ordinary people and horticulturists as much as botanists, valued for their unrivaled flower beauty and enthralling charm.

The family Orchidaceae, one of the largest and most diverse plant families in the world, with over 28,000 species distributed across various ecosystems (POWO, 2025). In India, orchids hold a special placc in floral diversity, with more than 1,250 recorded species (Singh *et al*, 2019; Agarwala *et al.*, 2023). Telangana, despite its predominantly dry and deciduous landscape, supports a surprising number of orchids (**35 species**), many of which thrive in the moist pockets of forests, riverine habitats, and hill ranges.

Telangana State: Geography and Climate

Telangana State, located in the central part of the eastern Deccan Plateau in India, covers an area of 114,840 square kilometers. Its topography is characterized by two primary regions: the Eastern Ghats and the plains, interspersed with low depressions. The Eastern Ghats are prominent in districts like Nagarkurnool, Nalgonda, Khammam, and Bhadradri Kothagudem.

Geographically, Telangana lies between 15°50′ and 19°55′ North latitudes and 77°14′ and 78°50′ East longitudes (Figure 1). It is bordered by Maharashtra to the north and northwest, Karnataka to the west, Chhattisgarh to the northeast, Odisha to the east, and Andhra Pradesh to the south. The state is drained by the Godavari and Krishna rivers, with a significant portion of their catchment areas falling within Telangana. However, much of the land is arid.

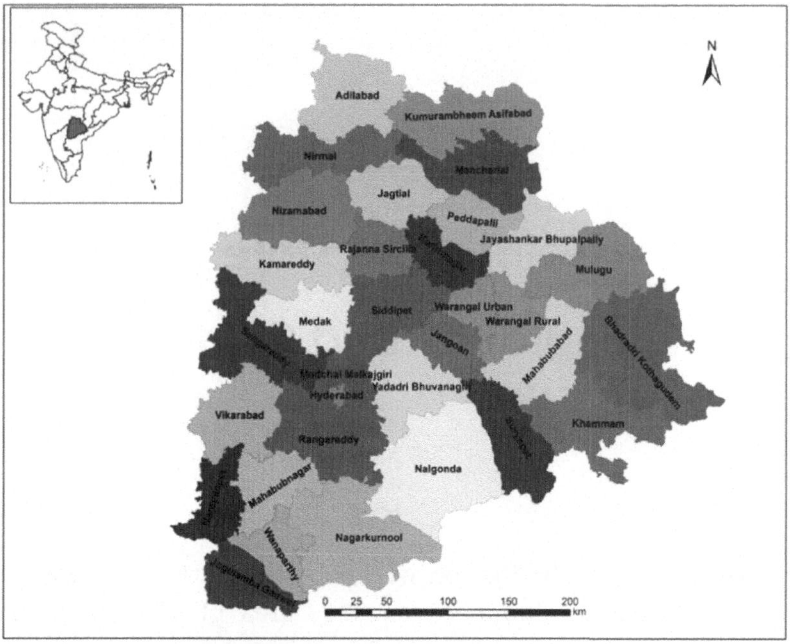

Figure 1. *Study area map- Telangana State*

The state's landscape is primarily an extensive plateau with an average elevation of 400 meters above sea level. This plateau is categorized into three erosional surfaces: above 600 meters, 300-450 meters, and 150-300 meters. The first surface, around Hyderabad, extends to the northwest and northeast. The second, covering a large central area, consists of rounded flat hills and rolling plains, primarily composed of granite. The third surface lies between the Godavari through to the east and west.

Telangana is rich in mineral resources, including extensive coal deposits excavated by the Singareni Collieries Company, limestone used in cement factories, and deposits of bauxite and mica.

The climate of Telangana is semi-arid, with hot and dry conditions predominating. Summers, from March to May, see average high temperatures around 42°C. The monsoon season, from June to September, brings approximately 755 mm of rainfall.

Winters, from late November to early February, are dry and mild, with average temperatures between 22-23°C.

The state experiences a monsoon-type tropical climate. Northern Telangana has a tropical rainy climate with mean daily temperatures above 20°C and annual rainfall of 150-200 cm. Southern Telangana has a hot steppe climate with mean daily temperatures around 18°C or less. Temperatures increase from west to east in December, with western districts experiencing temperatures below 20°C, central zones between 20-22°C, and eastern areas above 22°C. May is the hottest month, with temperatures reaching 45°C in northeastern and eastern regions.

Geology, Soil and Rivers of Telangana

Telangana's geology is diverse, featuring formations from the oldest Dharwar schists to recent alluvium. The Archaean gneissic and granite complex dominates the rock formations. Districts like Adilabad, Nizamabad, Medak, Warangal, and Khammam have various rock systems, including igneous and partly metamorphosed rocks, rich in iron, copper, asbestos, barites, limestone, and steatite.

Dharwar formations extend into Mahabubnagar district, containing significant minerals. Archaean or Peninsular gneisses, composed of granites, granodiorites, and banded gneisses, are prevalent. Puranas, including limestone, sandstones, slates, and shales, are found in Mahabubnagar, Nalgonda, Ranga Reddy and Adilabad districts.

Gondwana formations, along the Pranahita and Godavari rivers, are the main repositories of Gondwana rocks. Lower Gondwana formations contain coal seams, exploited in Kothagudem, Yellandu, Bellampalli, and Godavari Khani. Upper Gondwana formations consist mainly of shales and sandstones along the Godavari trough. Deccan trap formations, composed of basaltic rocks with limestone interbeds, are found in western and northwestern areas. Laterites occur as caps over Deccan traps in western Telangana.

Telangana's soil types are broadly classified into red, black, and laterite soils. Red soils, derived from gneisses and granite, are poor in nitrogen but have medium to high potash. They cover large areas, including Karimnagar, Warangal, Nizamabad, Mahabubnagar, Nalgonda, and Khammam districts. Black soils, rich in calcium and potash but poor in nitrogen, are found in western and northwestern regions. Deep black soils are present along the Pranahita, Godavari, and Krishna rivers, while light black soils, derived from Deccan trap rocks, are in Adilabad, Ranga Reddy, Medak, and Nizamabad districts. Mixed red and black soils are found between the Krishna and Godavari rivers, with fertility varying by elevation. Laterite soils, formed by the decomposition of gneisses, are poor in organic matter and nutrients. They occur in parts of Sangareddy, Vikarabad, Ranga Reddy, and Hyderabad districts.

Telangana, known as a "river state," is dominated by the Godavari and Krishna rivers and their tributaries. The Godavari, originating in the Western Ghats, flows for 720 km within Telangana, receiving water from tributaries like Kadam, Pranahita, Manjira, and Penganga. The Krishna, also originating in the Western Ghats, flows for 338 km through Telangana, with the Moosi as its main tributary. The Manjira, a major tributary of the Godavari, flows through Sangareddy district. The state also features numerous tanks and lakes, like Pakhal, Ramappa, and Lakkavaram, and waterfalls such as Pochera, Kuntala, and Bogatha.

Forests, Vegetation and Wildlife in Telangana

Forests play a crucial role in Telangana's economy, providing timber, fuel wood, bamboo, beedi leaf, and other products. However, deforestation, driven by natural causes and human activities like mining, dam construction, and overgrazing, has become a significant concern.

Telangana's forest area covers 24.05% of its geographical area, with most forests being reserved. High forest cover is found in northern districts like Adilabad, Asifabad, Khammam, and in the Eastern Ghats. Districts like Medak, Nalgonda, Ranga Reddy, and Hyderabad have low forest cover.

Telangana's vegetation is diverse, influenced by climate, soil, and altitude. The major forest types, as per Champion and Seth, 1968 classification, include:

- **Tropical Moist Deciduous Forests:** Found along rivers and streams, featuring species like *Terminalia arjuna* and *Syzygium cumini.*
- **Southern Dry Deciduous Forests:** Widespread, with species like *Tectona grandis* and *Anogeissus latifolia.*
- **Northern Mixed Dry Deciduous Forests:** Occurring at higher elevations, with species like *Albizia amara* and *Hardunckia binat*a.

- **Dry Savannah Forests:** Resulting from biotic interference, scattered in Mahabubnagar and Khammam districts.
- **Tropical Scrub Forests:** Found in arid zones, featuring drought-resistant shrubs and trees.

These diverse ecosystems contribute to Telangana's rich biodiversity and ecological significance.

Telangana, with its diverse landscapes and rich biodiversity, is home to a fascinating array of orchids. These delicate and enchanting flowers, often hidden within dense forests, along riverbanks, or clinging to rocky outcrops, play a crucial role in the region's ecological balance. Despite their beauty and significance, orchids remain one of the least understood plant groups in Telangana.

Pullaiah (2015) has reported 7 genera and 12 species of orchids from Telangana; Reddy & Reddy (2016) have reported 15 genera and 20 species. Present study revealed 15 genera and 35 species.

Orchids of Telangana State: A Pictorial Guide for Identification is designed to bridge this knowledge gap by providing a visual and scientific reference for researchers, nature enthusiasts, and conservationists. This book is structured as a pictorial guide to aid in the easy identification of orchids found in Telangana. Each species is presented with high-resolution photographs, a brief botanical description, habitat details, and flowering season information. The visual approach ensures that even non-specialists, such as students, amateur botanists, and nature lovers can appreciate and recognize different orchid species without requiring much taxonomic knowledge.

Moreover, this guide serves as a useful tool for conservationists and policymakers by providing insights into the distribution of orchids in Telangana. Understanding the diversity of these plants is crucial for developing effective conservation strategies, especially for species that are rare, endemic, or threatened.

Significance of Orchids in Telangana

Orchids are not just aesthetically appealing; they play a vital role in the ecosystem and traditional medicine. Many orchid species form symbiotic relationships with fungi, contributing to soil health and biodiversity. Some are used in Ayurveda and traditional medicine for their medicinal properties, while others are prized for their ornamental value. However, habitat destruction, deforestation and climate change pose significant threats to their survival. Documenting and studying these species are essentially required for their conservation.

Who Can Use This Guide?

This book is designed for a wide range of readers, including Botanists and Researchers, for taxonomic studies and biodiversity assessments; Students and Educators, as a reference for academic studies in plant sciences and conservation biology; Nature Enthusiasts and Photographers, to explore and appreciate the beauty of Telangana's orchids and Forest and Wildlife Officials, to aid in biodiversity conservation and habitat protection efforts. Moreover, it will meet the needs of all categories of people in basic identification of orchids dwelling in the state of Telengana.

By combining scientific accuracy with visual appeal, this guide aims to make orchid identification an engaging and rewarding experience. We hope that this book foster a deeper appreciation for Telangana's orchid diversity and encourage efforts to document, conserve and protect these botanical treasures for future generations.

Orchid Morphology

The Orchidaceae family, renowned for its exceptionally beautiful flowers, exhibits remarkable species diversity. This variation is evident in the size, shape, and structure of both vegetative and floral characteristics, as well as in flower color and fragrance. Predominantly perennial herbaceous plants, orchids thrive on diverse substrates as terrestrials, epiphytes, and saprophytes. Typical orchid structures include roots, stems, pseudobulbs, rhizomes, tubers, corms, leaves, inflorescences, flowers, pedicels, ovaries, labella, columns, anthers, stigmatic cavities, rostellum, pollinia, capsules and seeds.

1. Terrestrial Orchids:

- These orchids grow naturally in soil, featuring aerial, leafy, and flowering shoots alongside underground structures like tubers, bulbs, or corms.
- These underground parts specialize in food and water conservation for vegetative propagation. Terrestrial orchids inhabit regions from the tropics to alpine zones.
- They often undergo extended periods of dormancy, completing their aerial life cycle with stems, leaves, flowers, and fruits during favorable seasons.
- With the exception of *Vanilla*, terrestrial orchids exhibit sympodial growth.

- Examples include genera such as *Eulophia, Habenaria and Zeuxine.*

2. Mycoheterotrophic Orchids:

- These orchids lack typical green leaves and rely on decaying organic matter for sustenance.
- They obtain nutrients from dead and decaying substances through mycorrhizal fungi in their roots, as they lack root hairs.
- Their roots contain a higher concentration of mycorrhiza compared to other orchid species.
- Examples include *Aphyllorchis montana, Epipogium aphyllum, and Galeola lindleyana* (orchids of this category are not reported so far from Telengana).

3. Epiphytic Orchids:

- These orchids grow on the trunks and branches of other plants without extracting nutrients or harming the host.
- Over half of all orchid species are epiphytic.
- They derive nutrition from humus accumulated on the substrate. They flourish in both tropical and temperate regions.
- Epiphytic orchids exhibit two growth forms:
    - Sympodial: Successive new growths originate from the base of the preceding one (e.g. *Dendrobium, Coelogyne*).
    - Monopodial: Elongated stems with a terminal growing apex, capable of reaching significant lengths (e.g. *Vanda*).

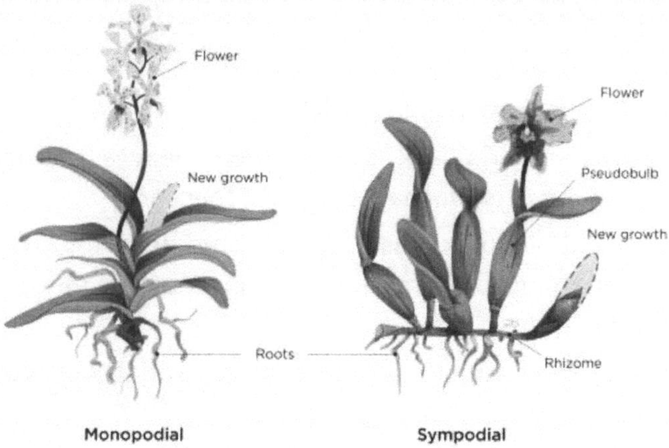

Source: https://espacepourlavie.ca/

Roots: Orchid roots display diverse morphologies, ranging from filiform and slender to thick and woolly. They serve multiple functions, including anchorage, water absorption, storage, and photosynthesis. They also facilitate a symbiotic relationship with mycorrhizal fungi.

Stems: Orchid stems vary in form, from thin and wiry to soft and succulent. They can be normal or modified into rhizomes, corms, or pseudobulbs. Terrestrial and monopodial epiphytic orchids possess normal stems, varying in size. Rhizomes are horizontal or ascending stems found in sympodial orchids. Corms are underground storage stems. Pseudobulbs, thickened or swollen stems, are primarily found in sympodial epiphytes.

Leaves: Orchid leaves are predominantly distichous and cauline. They can range from single leaves to numerous leaves, or may be reduced to scales or entirely absent. Leaf shapes include convolute, conduplicate, and cylindrical. Leaf margins are typically entire, and apices vary in shape. Most orchid leaves are glabrous, though some genera have hairy leaves. Leaves are typically green with parallel venation, but some exhibit mottling or variegation. Leaf shapes can be dorsiventrally flattened, terete, or equitant.

Inflorescence: Orchid inflorescences are typically racemes, which may be branched (paniculate), spicate, capitate, corymbose, cymose, or verticillate. Inflorescence placement varies: axillary in monopodial orchids, terminal in most terrestrial orchids, and terminal/sub-terminal in sympodial epiphytes. The number of flowers ranges from solitary to hundreds. Peduncles and rachises can be erect or pendulous, and flowers can be arranged in various patterns. Leaf bearing and flower bearing stems can be seperate.

Flowers: Orchid flowers exhibit a wide range of variation in form, size, shape, color, and fragrance. Sizes range from a few millimeters to 100-150 mm. Colors vary from light to vibrant. Flowers are typically zygomorphic and trimerous. Components include floral bracts, petals, sepals, columns, pedicels, ovaries, stigmatic cavities, rostellums, anthers, and pollinia. Floral bracts have varied characteristics. The ovary is inferior and continuous with the pedicel. Sepals and petals form the perianth, which may be free or partially fused. The labellum, or lip, is a modified petal that varies significantly in shape and size. The column, or gynostemium, is formed by the fusion of the style, stigma, and stamen. The stigma is typically three-lobed. The rostellum prevents self-pollination. Anthers typically contain pollinia, masses of pollen grains. Pollinia vary in shape, size, and texture. The pollinarium is the compound structure formed by the pollinia, caudicle, stipe, and viscidium.

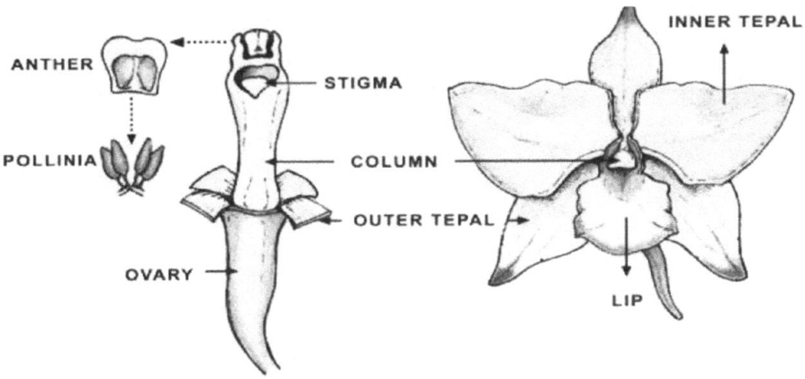

Schematic diagram of an orchid flower (source: Serena Aceto)

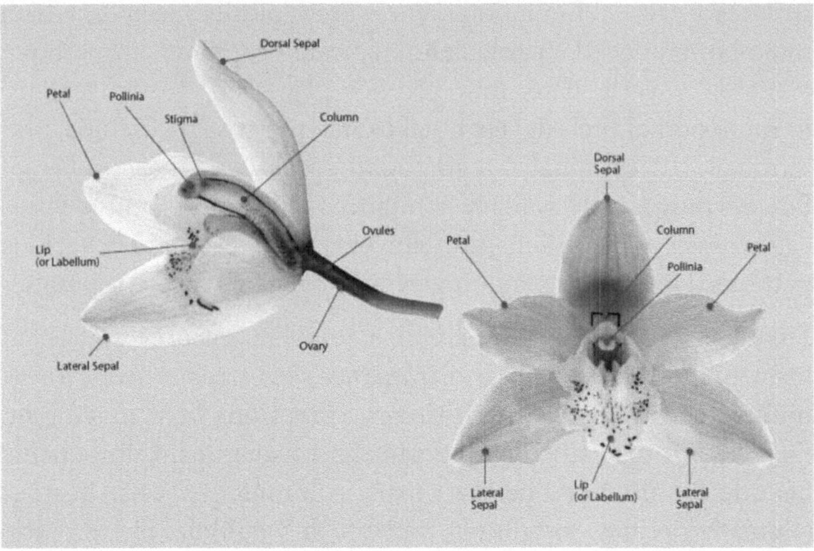

Orchid flower parts (source: www.nybg.org)

Fruits: Orchid ovaries develop into capsules after fertilization. Capsules vary in shape, size, and texture. They can be fusiform, clavate, obovoid, ellipsoidal, oblong, cylindrical, or globular.

Seeds: Orchid seeds are among the smallest of all flowering plants. They are dust-like and contain an undifferentiated embryo. A single capsule can contain millions of seeds. Seeds are typically fusiform or elliptic and winged, adapted for wind dispersal.

Socio-Economic importance

Orchids in Telangana occur sporadically and being herbaceous plants, escaped from the attentions of the common man. For this reason they have no noticeable socio-economic use unlike many other plants. Orchids, nevertheless are known for their showy flowers. They are cared world over for their high floricultural value. Several orchids also possess therapeutic value.

1. Floricultural importance of orchids

Orchids have a unique quality to breed freely to form hybrids. Florists have used this property to their advantage in creating through selective breeding a stupendously large number- nearly 1,50,000 hybrids. These hybrids often surpass the parents in the quality of flowers and are in great demand among the flower lovers. Orchid cut-flower trade is in practice in several countries like Thailand, Singapore etc; the main marketing is in U.S.A, Japan, and Netherlands etc. In India in general and in Telangana in particular commercial use of orchids is almost negligible.

Presently in international arena there is a growing demand of orchids in floriculture industry in terms of cut-flowers especially in cities and people have shown interest to cultivate orchids. Orchid farming is low-volume, less laborious and yet is of high value and remunerative. Now, slowly orchid farming is getting popularized in remote areas also. By this the increasing demand of orchid cut-flowers will be materialized to a great extent.

2. Therapeutic importance of orchids

Orchids (wild) have immense medicinal value. In the Indian system of medicine several ingredients like *Gandhaharini, Jeevak, Jeevanti, Kakoli, Munjattak, Rasna, Riddhis, Swarnajeewanti* and *Vriddhi,* are all orchids. These contain phyto-constituents like alkaloids, flavonoids, glycosides and terpens etc. of therapeutic importance and possess anti-bacterial, anti-viral, anti-malarial, etc. properties. Orchids of Telangana with therapeutic value, as depicted from number of literature, are given in the below table.

Table 2 - *Medicinal use of Orchids of Telangana*

Sl. No.	Botanical name	Habit	Therapeutic use
1	*Acampe praemorsa*	E	Root paste along with tubers of *Asparagus racemosus* is administered in arthritis and rheumatism.
2	*Cymbidium aloifolium*	E	Salep made from pseudobulb is used as nutrient and demulcent; as emetic and purgative. Decoction of plant is used to stop vomiting and diarrhea. Plant is used in treatment of tumor. Root powder is used in paralysis.
3	*Eulophia graminea*	T	Pseudobulb juice used as ear-drop.
4	*Eulophia picta* (=*Geodorum densiflorum*)	T	Extract of corm is antidiarrheal; also used in skin inflammation and tumors. Root paste is useful in curing irregular menstrual cycle in women.

5	*Habenaria marginata*	T	Boiled plant extract is used in suppressed urination. Tubers are used in the treatment of malignant ulcer.
6	*Vanda tesellata*	E	In rheumatism; in nervous disorder; in scorpion bite; in asthma; anti-malarial. Decoction of root given for cholera; paste of roots applied on body to reduce fever.

Where to get orchids from

Orchid plants may be availed from an authentic nursery man who has his stock from laboratory raised plants. They should never be purchased from persons who have collected the plants from the wild. These days many big nurseries in South India in Chennai, Bangaluru, Thiruvananthapuram have come up who are dealing with tissue culture-raised orchid seedlings in commercial scale. Local nursery men procure their requirement from such firms.

Selection of Plants for raising in household garden

Hybrid orchids are the right choice for ones possession. Beginners may insist such plants which are warm-loving; they require no elaborate houses for rearing them. Besides plants with different flowering plants should be selected, so that at any point of time a few plants are in flower. Large size, brightly coloured, longer lasting are other points to be looked into while purchasing the plants.

Selection of Plants for raising in household garden

Orchids can be raised in a corner of the garden where a small net-house about 3 m high can be located. This may be erected with a frame work from light steel angles and flat or G. I. pipes. The top may be spread with agronet of 75% shade; this net may be extended to hang on the sides for about 1.5 m. covering part of the sides of the net house. The lower half may be kept open or enclosed with G. I. woven wire (chain-link). A few long benches fabricated with M.S. angle, frame and the top with slotted steel sheet, may be arranged inside the net house for keeping the flower-pots. Orchids love a raised position with good ventilation. The floor may be paved with bricks laid over sand and the joints cement-pointed.

Containers and growing media

The epiphytic orchids are grown in small (10-15cm) perforated clay or plastic pots. The potting medium consists of brick pieces broken to about 25 mm size. Neatly cut coconut husks of similar size could also be admixed.

Potting method

The pots may be filled to about 2/3 depth with the potting material. A slender bamboo stalk may be kept at the centre and the plant is placed close to it. The rest part of the pot should then be filled with potting material leasing some margin from the top. The plant may be tied to the stalk and the potting material pressed by both palms from margin to centre of the pot. It is now ready for placing on the bench.

Watering

Orchid plants should be well watered daily. Over-watering should however be avoided. A P.V.C. hose pipe with a sprinkler head may be used, so that the whole plant gets a thorough bath. If it is convenient otherwise, misting device may be provided inside the house. Slender P.V.C. pipes with misting points and a pumping device are all that are required for this. This arrangement is essential in plain areas like ours where the temperature remains high and sometimes very high in summer. A temperature range of 25° - 30° C and 60-70% relative humidity is ideal for growing many popular hybrid general of orchids like *Dendrobium, Vanda* etc.

Feeding

Raising orchids in pots need feeding. Organic manure, such as decanted and diluted fresh cow-dung, is very popular. Inorganic manure is however mostly used. This consists of standard fertilizers of NPK (20:20:20) supplemented intermittently with micro-nutrients. NPK is marketed under various names, the common being 'Sufala'. Feeding may be done once a week through spray early morning after regular watering. The dose is 0.2% concentration (2 gms of fertilizer in one litre of water) in summer and rains and 0.1% concentration in winter.

Plant Protection

Attack from insects, pests and fungi is to be watched. Periodic spray (through a fine nozzle) of insecticides, pesticides and fungicides prevents attacks and diseases. Insecticides like 'Sumathion' or 'Lannate' at 1 ml per litre be applied on alternate weeks. For slugs and snails 'Metaldehyde' of similar concentration may be applied as and when required. Bactericide like 'Agrimycin' at 2 gm per litre may be applied monthly. Fungicides like 'Dithane', 'Captan' etc. of the above concentration may be applied once a month and in rainy season at two weeks interval. The best preventive against such attacks is to keep the growing area, the growth media and of course the plants clean.

Vegetative Propagation of Orchids

Vegetative propagation is suitable for orchids like *Cymbidium, Dendrobium,* etc. When a well-established plant overgrows its container, at should divided for better growth condition. The creeping stem buried in the potting medium can be out and the tufted plant split into small clumps and potted in new pots. Dendrobiums develop offshoots on their stem known as 'keikies'. These 'keikies' could be planted in separate pots while still connected to the mother plant. Once the new roots save spread in the potting media the offshoots can be separated from the mother plants.

The best time for repotting is usually May-June immediately after flowering and the current seasons new plants come up with new roots. Care should be taken while separating so that the new shoots and root tips are not damaged.

Conservation

The orchids have undergone severe threat of extinction by gradual decrease in their population in the wild. This is mainly due to both biotic as well as abiotic factors. The major causes are habitat loss due to forest clearance to cater the ever increasing greed of the human beings, shifting cultivation, forest fires, rapid march of urbanization, un-judicious exploitation of orchids without knowing the status of orchid species. Climate change also plays a significant role in depletion of orchids coupled with changes in the micro-climatic conditions.

Orchids are important for their potential horticultural value and therapeutic usages. As the most advanced as well as primitive family among the flowering plants, they have various uses in the field of plant genetics. They are good indicator species; presence of orchids depicts the health of local forest ecosystem. It is therefore, essential to conserve orchids. For successful and effective conservation protection of habitats are highly required as orchids are habitat specific plants thus cannot be conserved in isolation. For conservation orchid-rich habitats, including whole forest, or a forest block with favourable micro-climates dwelling with a sizable population of rare orchids, should be declared as a botanical reserve, or a protectorate. Orchid sanctuaries should be established. Large scale plantation of host trees like 'Kusum' (*Schleichera oleosa*), 'Jamun' (*Syzygium cumuni*),

'Mango' (*Mangifera indica*), 'Mahua' (*Madhuca indica*) etc, will contribute significantly towards the conservation of orchids especially epiphytes. Orchids being the small plants or more appropriately herbs their conservation is always over looked by conservationists and scientific populace, as all are concerned for large trees. Conservation of orchids should also be attempted *ex-situ* in botanical gardens, parks, and tourist resorts etc. Awareness should be generated among the plant lovers, forest employees and also general public about the orchids, their role in the eco-system and necessity of their conservation. This will supplement to the *in-situ* conservations of orchids.

Table: 1. *Check List of Orchids of Telangana*

No.	Scientific Name	Habit
1	*Acampe praemorsa* (Roxb.) Blatt. & McCann	Epiphyte
2	*Aerides multiflora* Roxb.	Epiphyte
3	*Coelogyne pallida* (Lindl.) Rchb.f.	Epiphyte
4	*Crepidium versicolor* (Lindl.) Sushil K. Singh, Agrawala & Jalal	Terrestrial
5	*Cymbidium aloifolium* (L.) Sw.	Epiphyte
6	*Dendrobium herbaceum* Lindl.	Epiphyte
7	*Dendrobium macrostachyum* Lindl.	Epiphyte
8	*Eulophia epidendraea* (J. Koenig ex Retz.) C.E.C. Fisch	Terrestrial
9	*Eulophia flava* (Lindl.) Hook.f.	Terrestrial
10	*Eulophia graminea* Lindl.	Terrestrial
11	*Eulophia nuda* Lindl.	Terrestrial
12	*Eulophia picta* (R.Br.) Ormerod	Terrestrial
13	*Eulophia recurva* (Roxb.) M. W. Chase, Kumar & Schuit.	Terrestrial

14	*Habenaria commelinifolia* (Roxb.) Wall. ex Lindl.	Terrestrial
15	*Habenaria furcifera* Lindl.	Terrestrial
16	*Habenaria hollandiana* Santapau	Terrestrial
17	*Habenaria marginata* Colebr.	Terrestrial
18	*Habenaria multicaudata* Sedgw.	Terrestrial
19	*Habenaria panigrahiana* S. Misra	Terrestrial
20	*Habenaria plantaginea* Lindl.	Terrestrial
21	*Habenaria ramayyana* Ram. Chary & J. J. Wood	Terrestrial
22	*Habenaria roxburghii* Nicolson	Terrestrial
23	*Habenaria thailandica* Seidenf.	Terrestrial
24	*Liparis deflexa* Hook.f.	Terrestrial
25	*Luisia zeylanica* Lindl.	Epiphyte
26	*Nervilia concolor* (Blume) Schltr.	Terrestrial
27	*Oberonia ensiformis* (Sm.) Lindl.	Epiphyte
28	*Oberonia wightiana* Lindl.	Epiphyte
29	*Peristylus goodyeroides* (D.Don) Lindl.	Terrestrial
30	*Peristylus lawii* Wight	Terrestrial
31	*Spathoglottis plicata* Blume	Terrestrial
32	*Vanda tessellata* (Roxb.) Hook. ex G. Don	Epiphyte
33	*Vanda testacea* (Lindl.) Rchb.f.	Epiphyte
34	*Zeuxine longilabris* (Lindl.) Trimen	Terrestrial
35	*Zeuxine strateumatica* (L.) Schltr.	Terrestrial

Species Enumeration

1. Acampe praemorsa

(Roxb.) Blatt. & McCann, J. Bombay Nat. Hist. Soc. 35: 495. 1932.

Epiphyte, rarely lithophytic, tufted. Stem woody, sheathed, erect, 15-30 cm high. Leaves alternate, distichous, narrowly oblong and unequally bilobed at apex, mucronate. Inflorescence short, condensed, axillary or leaf opposed, sub-umbellate, sheathed with sterile bracts; bracts ovate, obtuse, margin serrate, brown, persistent. Flowers clustered, petals and sepals fleshy, succulent, creamy yellow with brown transverse lining and spots. Lip white with irregular transverse violet markings, on both upper and lower surfaces, 3-lobed, base saccate. Lateral lobes small, narrow, erect, thick; mid lobe fleshy, ovate, truncate, feebly bilobed at the apex.

Flowering & Fruiting: May-August.

Distribution in Telangana: Adilabad and Khammam Warangal.

Distribution in India: Telangana, Andhra Pradesh, Chhattisgarh, Dadara & Nagar Haveli, Daman & Diu, Goa, Gujarat, Jharkhand, Karnataka, Kerala, Madhya Pradesh, Maharashtra, Odisha, Rajasthan and Tamil Nadu.

Distribution in World: India, Bangladesh, Cambodia, China, Hainan, Laos, Malaya, Myanmar, Nepal, Philippines, Sri Lanka, Taiwan, Thailand and Vietnam

2. Aerides multiflora

Roxb. Pl. Coromandel 3: 68.1820.

An epiphyte. Stem 10-25 cm long. Leaves 15-20 cm long, crowded, obtuse, deeply channeled and keeled, variable in breadth. Racemes 15-30 cm long, rarely branched, shortly peduncled. Flowers 2-3 cm across, rose purple, sometimes spotted with darker. Sepals and petals sub-equal, oblong, tips rounded, odd sepal and petal ovate-oblong; lateral ones ovate-obovate; lip 3-lobed; median lobe triangular-cordate, with a narrowed, rounded top, violet-red; spur straight, obtuse, upcurved; column beaked; anther long-beaked, strap long, slender. Capsules subclavate, stoutly pedicelled.

Flowering & Fruiting: March-August.

Distribution in Telangana: Khammam.

Distribution in India: Telangana, Andaman & Nicobar Islands, Andhra Pradesh, Arunachal Pradesh, Assam, Chhattisgarh, Karnataka, Madhya Pradesh, Manipur, Meghalaya, Mizoram, Nagaland, Odisha, Sikkim, Tripura, Uttarakhand and West Bengal.

Distribution in World: India, Bangladesh, Bhutan, Cambodia, Laos, Myanmar, Nepal, Thailand and Vietnam

3. Coelogyne pallida

(Lindl.) Rchb.f., W.G.Walpers, Ann. Bot. Syst. 6: 288. 1861. (=*Pholidota pallida* Lindl., Edw. Bot. Reg. 21: subt. 1777. 1835.)

Epiphytic herb, pseudobulb aggregated, narrowly ovate-cylindric. Leaf solitary, elliptic-lanceolate or obovate-oblong, tapering into a short shout petiole, apex acute. Inflorescence terminal drooping racemes, densely many flowered. Flowers bifarious, creamish-white or pinkish. Floral bracts pale brown, persistent, longer than the slender stalked ovary. Petals oblong-ovate. Lip panduriform, 3-lobed; hypochile yellow, laterals hatchet-shaped or broadly oblong-rounded, mid lobe 2-lobulate, lobules quadrate-suborbicular. Pollinia 4, ovoid-pyriform. Column winged, stigmatic surface funnel-shaped. Capsules ellipsoid.

Flowering & Fruiting: June-December.

Distribution in Telangana: Khammam.

Distribution in India: Telangana, Andhra Pradesh, Arunachal Pradesh, Assam, Jharkhand, Manipur, Meghalaya, Nagaland, Sikkim, and West Bengal.

Distribution in World: India, Cambodia, China, Laos, Myanmar, Nepal, Thailand and Vietnam.

4. Crepidium versicolor

(Lindl.) Sushil K. Singh, Agrawala & Jalal (=*Malaxis versicolor* (Lindl.) Abeyw., Ceylon J. Sci., Biol. Sci. 2: 83. 1959.)

Terrestrial herb, features annular, elongated pseudobulbs. Leaves broadly ovate or ovate-elliptic, thinly membranous, acute or acuminate, pliated, silvery or purplish. Inflorescence a dense, many-flowered raceme. Floral bracts green, deflexed, ovate-lanceolate, acuminate. Flowers non-resupinate, fragrant, green or yellowish-purple. Lip reniform, pectinately toothed margins. Column greenish-yellow, oblong-ovate. Stigma obovate-oblong. Pollinia 4, pyriform. Capsule obovate-oblong.

Flowering & Fruiting: September-October.

Distribution in Telangana: Karimnagar and Khammam.

Distribution in India: Telangana, Andhra Pradesh, Goa, Karnataka, Kerala, Maharashtra, Odisha and Tamil Nadu.

Distribution in World: India and Sri Lanka.

5. Cymbidium aloifolium

(L.) Sw., Nova Acta Regiae Soc. Sci. Upsal., ser. 2, 6: 73. 1799.

Epiphytic herb. Pseudobulbs laterally compressed. Leaves linear, oblong, curved, fleshy, notched at the apex. Inflorescence raceme, decurved, arising from the base. Flowers yellow with brown stripes and brownish lip. Bracts minute, much shorter than ovary. Lip as long as the sepals, oblong, 3-lobed, saccate at the base, lateral lobes acute, longer than the column, mid-lobe ovate-oblong, decurved, striped with pink or purple.

Flowering & Fruiting: February-November.

Distribution in Telangana: Khammam.

Distribution in India: Telangana, Andaman & Nicobar Islands, Arunachal Pradesh, Andhra Pradesh, Assam, Bihar, Chhattisgarh, Goa, Jharkhand, Karnataka, Kerala, Madhya Pradesh, Maharashtra, Manipur, Meghalaya, Mizoram, Nagaland, Odisha, Sikkim, Tamil Nadu, Tripura, Uttarakhand, Uttar Pradesh and West Bengal.

Distribution in World: India, Bangladesh, Bhutan, Cambodia, China, Jawa, Laos, Malaysia, Myanmar, Nepal, Sri Lanka, Sumatera, Thailand and Vietnam

6. Dendrobium herbaceum

Lindl., Edwards's Bot. Reg. 26(Misc.): 69. 1840.

Epiphytic herb, pendulous, up to 1 m tall. Stems much-branched, lower portion devoid of leaves (leafless). Leaves caducous, linear-lanceolate, apex acute to subobtuse. Inflorescence a terminal raceme, 2-3-flowered, rarely exceeding 2.5 cm. Flowers yellow. Pedicels filiform. Bracts lanceolate, scarious. Sepals lateral sepals oblong-lanceolate, slightly falcate, base broadened; dorsal sepal oblong-lanceolate, apex rounded. Petals linear, obtuse. Spur minute. Lip oblong, slightly constricted apically; side lobes very narrow or obsolete; midlobe ovate, subacute, margin entire, ellipsoid, base tapering.

Flowering & Fruiting: August-December.

Distribution in Telangana: Khammam

Distribution in India: Telangana, Andhra Pradesh, Chhattisgarh, Goa, Jharkhand, Karnataka, Kerala, Madhya Pradesh, Maharashtra, Mizoram, Odisha, Sikkim, Tamil Nadu and West Bengal.

Distribution in World: India and Bangladesh.

7. Dendrobium macrostachyum

Lindl., Gen. Sp. Orchid. Pl.: 78. 1830.

Epiphytic herbs. Pseudobulbs slender, pendulous. Leaves sessile, sub-falcate ovate-lanceolate, sub-acuminate, thick, caduceus. Inflorescence solitary or in cymes, peduncle solitary or in pair from the nodes of the leafless stem. Flowers not much spreading lemon green, inodorous. Bracts oblong-truncate. Lip convolute throughout the length, edge fimbriate-serrate except towards the base and its wavy apex, yellowish with reddish purple veins.

Flowering & Fruiting: April-September.

Distribution in Telangana: Nagarkurnool.

Distribution in India: Telangana, Andaman and Nicobar Islands, Arunachal Pradesh, Goa, Jharkhand, Karnataka, Kerala, Madhya Pradesh, Maharashtra, Odisha, Tamil Nadu, Uttarakhand and West Bengal.

Distribution in World: India, Bangladesh, Borneo, Jawa, Lesser Sunda Is., Malaya, Maldives, Myanmar, Nepal, Queensland, Sri Lanka, Sulawesi, Sumatera, Thailand and Vietnam.

8. Eulophia epidendraea

(J. Koenig ex Retz.) C.E.C. Fisch., J. S. Gamble, Fl. Madras: 1434. 1928.

A terrestrial herb. Stem pseudobulbous, covered with membranous, basal sheaths. Leaves many, linear, 16-50 x 0.8-1.6 cm, acuminate, keeled, 5-8-veined. Racemes 40 cm long. Flowers ash-green with membranous, sterile bracts; floral bracts ovate, acute. Dorsal sepal lanceolate-oblong; laterals obovate-lanceolate; petals broadly lanceolate; lip oblong; lateral lobes of lip small, erect embracing the column; mid lobe broad, oblong-round, recurved; disc with 5-8 ridges; spur short, cylindrical, with purple dots and parallel to the ovary; anther terminal, 2-loculed; pollinia 2, globose, depressed towards the base and connected to large, disciform gland by a short, tongue-shaped strap.

Flowering & Fruiting: February-August.

Distribution in Telangana: Khammam.

Distribution in India: Telangana, Andaman & Nicobar Islands, Andhra Pradesh, Chhattisgarh, Karnataka, Kerala, Maharashtra, Odisha, Tamil Nadu, Uttarakhand and West Bengal.

Distribution in World: India, Bangladesh and Sri Lanka.

9. Eulophia flava

(Lindl.) Hook.f., Fl. Brit. India 6: 7. 1890. (=*E. cullenii* (Wight) Blume, Coll. Orchid. 182. 1859.)

Terrestrial herb, up to 80 cm height, sprouting from brownish-white, flattened corms. Leaves 2-3 pleated, emerge post-flowering. Inflorescence, a lax raceme with numerous, sweet-scented, bright yellow flowers, each about 4 cm across. Floral bracts greenish-yellow, precede the flowers. Sepals distinct, 5-8 veined. Petals are broadly obovate, 3-lobed lip, with maroon-dotted striations, spur conical. Column yellowish-white, clavate. Capsules fusiform, 4 cm long.

Flowering & Fruiting: June-August.

Distribution in Telangana: Komurambheem Asifabad.

Distribution in India: Telangana, Andhra Pradesh, Bihar, Chhattisgarh, Jharkhand, Kerala, Madhya Pradesh, Odisha, Tamil Nadu, Uttarakhand and Uttar Pradesh.

Distribution in World: India, Cambodia, China, Hainan, Laos, Myanmar, Nepal, Thailand and Vietnam.

10. Eulophia graminea

Lindl., Gen. Sp. Orchid. Pl.: 182. 1833.

Terrestrial, erect herb, up to 65 cm in height, pseudobulbs above the ground, greenish brown, globose-ovoid to ovoid-conical. Leaves linear-lanceolate, acute-acuminate at apex. Inflorescence 1-3, erect with a few short branches, lax-flowered, up to 50 cm. Flowers 1.5-2 cm in diameter, olive-green color with maroon to purple-brown veins. Labellum oblong-obovate, distinctly 3-lobed; lateral lobes ovate-triangular; mid-lobe broadly obovate to suborbicular, with an undulate or crisped margin; disc centrally adorned with 3-5 crested, filiform, papillose lamellae; spur conical-cylindrical, incurved.

Flowering & Fruiting: March-May.

Distribution in Telangana: Mahabubnagar.

Distribution in India: Telangana, Arunachal Pradesh, Assam, Bihar, Jharkhand, Kerala, Madhya Pradesh, Maharashtra, Meghalaya, Mizoram, Nagaland, Odisha, Punjab, Sikkim, Tamil Nadu, Tripura, Uttar Pradesh, Uttarakhand and West Bengal.

Distribution in World: India, Bangladesh, Bhutan, Borneo, China, Indonesia, Japan, Loas, Malaysia, Myanmar, Nepal, Pakistan, Philippines, Singapore, Sri Lanka, Sumatra, United States of America (Florida), Vietnam, Taiwan and Thailand.

11. Eulophia nuda

Lindl., Gen. Sp. Orchid. Pl. 180. 1833. (=*E. spectabilis* Suresh in D. H. Nicolson, C. R. Suresh & K. S. Manilal, Interpr. Van Rheede's Hort. Malab. 300. 1988.)

Terrestrial herb up to 100 cm in height. Leaves oblong-lanceolate to elliptic-lanceolate, 20-55 x 1-12 cm, acuminate tip. Racemes, up to 80 cm long, 6-12 loosely arranged flowers, each 2.5-4.5 cm wide. Flowers, pink or greenish-maroon or greenish-maroon. Labellum, pale-green, pinkish white, obovate-oblong, obscurely 3-lobed. Disc features 2-11 thick lamellae, spur flattened, conical, obtuse apex. Pollinia oblong-ovoid, capsules fusiform.

Flowering & Fruiting: February-June.

Distribution in Telangana: Karimnagar.

Distribution in India: Telangana, Andaman & Nicobar Islands, Andhra Pradesh, Arunachal Pradesh, Assam, Bihar, Chhattisgarh, Goa, Jharkhand, Karnataka, Kerala, Madhya Pradesh, Maharashtra, Manipur, Meghalaya, Mizoram, Nagaland, Odisha, Punjab, Sikkim, Tamil Nadu, Tripura, Uttarakhand, Uttar Pradesh and West Bengal.

Distribution in World: India, Bangladesh, Bhutan, Borneo, China, Cambodia, Fiji, Indonesia, Japan, Java, Laos, Philippines, Malaysia, Myanmar, Nepal, New Guinea, Singapore, Sri Lanka, Thailand and Vietnam.

12. Eulophia picta

(R.Br.) Ormerod, Checkl. Papuasian Orchids: 293. 2017. (=*Geodorum densiflorum* (Lam.) Schltr., Repert. Spec. Nov. Regni Veg. Beih. 4: 259.1919.)

Terrestrial herb. Corm subterranean, tuberous, rhizomatous. Leaves cauline, unequal, smaller below, plicate, elliptic-lanceolate, acuminate, plicate, multiple veined. Inflorescence lateral, arising from the base of newly developed foliar shoot, taller than leaves, de-curved during flowering, erects during fruiting, green, terete, sheathed, sheaths lanceolate-ovate, acuminate. Floral bracts, green, narrowly lanceolate, acuminate, constricted at the base. Flower pinkish purple, not fully opened. Lip boat shaped, obscurely 3-lobed, margin deflexed, ventricose and thickened, with an incurved slit opening leading to nectar, lateral lobes broad, mid lobe crenulate, broadly bilobed.

Flowering & Fruiting: August-November.

Distribution in Telangana: Karimnagar and Nagarkurnool.

Distribution in India: Telangana, Andaman & Nicobar Islands, Andhra Pradesh, Arunachal Pradesh, Assam, Bihar, Chhattisgarh, Jharkhand, Karnataka, Kerala, Madhya Pradesh, Maharashtra, Manipur, Meghalaya, Mizoram, Nagaland, Odisha, Sikkim, Tamil Nadu, Tripura, Uttarakhand and West Bengal.

Distribution in World: India, Australia, Bangladesh, Bhutan, Cambodia, China, Fiji, Japan, Hong Kong, Loas, Malaysia, Myanmar, Nepal, Papua New Guinea, Sri Lanka, Taiwan, Thailand, Tonga and Vietnam.

13. Eulophia recurva

(Roxb.) M. W. Chase, Kumar & Schuit., Phytotaxa 491: 53. 2021. (=*Geodorum recurvum* (Roxb.) Alston, H. Trimen, Handb. Fl. Ceylon 6(Suppl.): 276. 1931.)

Terrestrial herb, up to 55 cm in height. Leaves sessile, narrowly elliptic-lanceolate, apex acute. Inflorescence lateral, shorter than the leaves, hooked at apex, bearing a dense raceme of 10-12 whitish-green flowers. Floral bracts, longer than the ovary, oblong-lanceolate and acuminate. Flowers 2-3 cm wide, sepals white, oblong-oblanceolate, petals white, obovate-lanceolate, acute. Lip sessile, cymbiform, undulate margins, truncate. The labellum, pale pink with a central yellow patch, is oblong-ovate. Column whitish-yellow, oblong-ovate, with a short foot. Stigma is quadrate, pollinia oblong-ovoid. Capsule spindle-shaped.

Flowering & Fruiting: May-September.

Distribution in Telangana: Nagarkurnool.

Distribution in India: Telangana, Andhra Pradesh, Assam, Jharkhand, Manipur, Odisha and West Bengal.

Distribution in World: India, Cambodia, China, Myanmar, Sri Lanka, Thailand and Vietnam.

14. Habenaria commelinifolia

(Roxb.) Wall. ex Lindl., Gen. Sp. Orchid. Pl.: 325. 1835.

Terrestrial herb, up to 90 cm high, tuberous geophyte, characterized by horizontal, cylindrical tubers. Leaves alternate, cauline, oblong-lanceolate, sheathing at base. Inflorescence spike, lax with many flowers; sterile bracts 3-5 cm long, lanceolate, acuminate, lower ones completely amplexicaul and upper ones semi-amplexicaul. Flowers white, scentless, 1.5-2 cm across Labellum 3-lobed, lobes filiform; spur 6 cm long, slender, clavate, apex greenish. Column elongated anther cells, trapezoidal pollinia with long caudicles. Capsule fusiform.

Flowering & Fruiting: September-November.

Distribution in Telangana: Mulugu.

Distribution in India: Telangana, Bihar, Chhattisgarh, Himachal Pradesh, Jammu & Kashmir, Jharkhand, Karnataka, Kerala, Madhya Pradesh, Maharashtra, Manipur, Odisha, Punjab, Sikkim, Uttarakhand, Uttar Pradesh and West Bengal.

Distribution in World: India, Myanmar, Nepal, Thailand and Vietnam.

15. Habenaria furcifera

Lindl., Gen. & Sp. Orchids: 319. 1835.

Terrestrial herb, up to 40 cm high, base of the stem covered with sheaths below the cluster of leaves. Leaves varying from narrow-elliptic to ovate-elliptic, slightly narrowed towards sheathing base, shiny, without any distinct margin. Inflorescence 20 cm long, erect, lax, many flowered. Flowers small pale to dark green, 1 cm across, very shortly pedicelled. Floral bracts are narrowly lanceolate. Sepals, 3-nerved, spreading or reflexed, dorsal sepal forming a hood with the petals. Petals oblong-lanceolate, forming a similar hood, lip 3-lobed from the base, side lobes filiform curved and divergent, mid lobe oblong, broad and straight. Column 2-3 mm, with small anthers and pollinia falcate ovoid. Stigma lobes short, elliptic. Spur slender, pendulous, 17-25 mm, surpasses the ovary. Capsules elliptic, ribbed, decurved.

Flowering & Fruiting: August-November.

Distribution in Telangana: Nagarkurnool.

Distribution in India: Telangana, Andhra Pradesh. Arunachal Pradesh. Assam. Bihar Chhattisgarh, Gujarat, Himachal Pradesh, Jammu & Kashmir, Jharkhand, Kerala, Madhya Pradesh, Maharashtra, Nagaland, Odisha, Punjab. Sikkim, Tamil Nadu, Uttarakhand, Uttar Pradesh and West Bengal.

Distribution in World: India, Bhutan, China, Myanmar, Nepal and Thailand.

16. Habenaria hollandiana

Santapau, Fl. Purandhar 126. 1957.

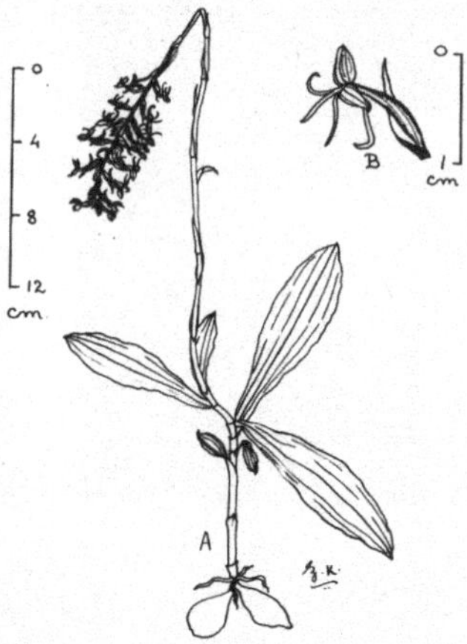

Terrestrial, tuberous herb, up to 60 cm high. Leaves simple, alternate, 3-5 clustered in the middle, elliptic-lanceolate, glabrous, acute or acuminate apex. Inflorescence in terminal racemes or cylindrical spikes, up to 50 cm. Flowers yellowish-green or white, 1-5 cm long. Bracts lanceolate or linear-lanceolate, papillose margins. Sepals subequal, ovate-oblong, obtuse. Petals as long as the sepals. Lip longer, featuring narrow side lobes exceeding the linear, obtuse mid lobe. Spur curved or incurved, 8 mm or shorter than the ovary. Pollinia 0.75 mm, Rostellum minute, 0.25 mm. Capsules, 2-3 cm long, beaked.

Flowering & Fruiting: September-November.

Distribution in Telangana: Nagarkurnool.

Distribution in India: Telangana, Andhra Pradesh, Jharkhand, Karnataka, Maharashtra and Tamil Nadu.

Distribution in World: India.

17. Habenaria marginata

Colebr., Exot. Fl.: t. 136. 1824

Terrestrial herb, up to 40 cm high. Tuberoids horizontal, oblong-ellipsoid. Leaves 2-5, clustered at the base, elliptic-lanceolate to oblong-lanceolate, obtuse, margin whitish-yellow. Inflorescence terminal, erect, spike cylindric, lax or dense flowered, with 5-14 flowers. Flowers golden yellow, inodorous, sessile, bracteate. Lip bright yellow, fleshy, trifurcate beyond the short claw, mid lobe linear, obtuse, slightly emarginated, in curled tips. Spur clavate, broad mouth.

Flowering & Fruiting: September-November.

Distribution in Telangana: Nagarkurnool.

Distribution in India: Telangana, Andhra Pradesh, Chhattisgarh, Dadra & Nagar Haveli, Daman & Diu, Goa, Gujarat, Himachal Pradesh, Jharkhand, Jammu & Kashmir, Karnataka, Kerala, Madhya Pradesh, Maharashtra, Meghalaya, Odisha, Punjab, Rajasthan, Tamil Nadu, Uttarakhand and West Bengal

Distribution in World: India, Bangladesh, Bhutan, China, Myanmar, Nepal and Thailand.

18. Habenaria multicaudata

Sedgw., Rec. Bot. Surv. India 6: 352. 1919.

Terrestrial herb, up to 65 cm high, with ovoid-ellipsoid tubers. Stem erect, greenish brown. Leaves simple, cauline, alternate, elliptic-oblong, margins entire or wavy, apex sub-acuminate or acute, clustered near the middle of the stem. Racemes 15 cm long, lax, shortly pedunculate, bracteates, with 10-15 flowers. Flowers pedicellate, bracteate, bracts sheathing. Sepals greenish-brown, unequal, 3-nerved, margins entire. Petals greenish-brown, bilobed; upper lobes linear-filiform, sub-falcate; lower segment, contorted. Lip greenish brown, longer than the sepals, spurred, trilobed, lobes unequal spreading, segments elongate, filiform, contorted; lateral longer than the mid lobe, up to 2.8 cm long, arched; mid lobe linear-filiform, straight. Spur 1.5 cm long, shorter than the ovary, ovary curved and swollen at apex. Capsule fusiform, ribbed.

Flowering & Fruiting: August-November.

Distribution in Telangana: Vikarabad.

Distribution in India: Telangana, Bihar, Goa, Karnataka, Kerala, Maharashtra and Tamil Nadu.

Distribution in World: India.

19. Habenaria panigrahiana

S. Misra, Blumea 27: 213. 1981.

Terrestrial herb, up to 35 cm high, features 1-2 globose or oblong tubers. Stems cylindric, leafy from base upwards. Leaves alternate, elliptic-lanceolate, base narrowed, margins undulate, apex acute. Inflorescence terminal, erect raceme, laxly 4 to 11- flowered. Flowers pale green, sweet-scented, about 3.4 cm across. Sepals sub-falcate. Petals bipartite to the base, upper segment sickle-shaped, cohering to the edge of dorsal sepal, narrowly linear-filiform. 2-veined. lower segment of petal longer than the upper segment, horizontal, apices incurved. Lip 3-lobed, narrowly linear-filiform lateral lobes, longer than the 1.2 cm, narrowly linear mid lobe. Spur narrowly cylindrical, column short. Ovary green, curved at apex. Stigmatic lobes oblong or clavate. Pollinia oblong or obovate. Capsules fusiform, 2.5 mm long.

Flowering & Fruiting: July-November.

Distribution in Telangana: Nagarkurnool.

Distribution in India: Telangana, Andhra Pradesh, Maharashtra, Odisha and Tamil Nadu.

Distribution in World: India.

20. Habenaria plantaginea

Lindl., Gen. Sp. Orchid. Pl.: 323. 1835.

Terrestrial herb, up to 35 cm high, features 1-2 tomentose, ovoid or ellipsoid tubers. Leaves radical, sessile, clustered at base, oblong-elliptic or oblong-lanceolate or obovate-oblong, acute at apex. Inflorescence racemose spikes densely many-flowered, 15 cm long, bracteate. Flowers white, 1.5 cm across, secund. Lip clawed, spreading, rhomboid, 3-lobed, lobes subacute, entire or toothed, lateral half ovate, mid lobe long, narrowly linear. Spur longer than the ovary, cylindrical, acute. Stigmatic lobes 2, clasping, elliptic-oblong. Pollinia 2, sub-globose. Capsules fusiform, 1.5 cm long, curved.

Flowering & Fruiting: August-October.

Distribution in Telangana: Nagarkurnool.

Distribution in India: Telangana, Andhra Pradesh, Arunachal Pradesh, Assam, Chandigarh, Chhattisgarh, Madhya Pradesh, Maharashtra, Haryana, Meghalaya, Himachal Pradesh, Jharkhand, Jammu & Kashmir, Karnataka, Kerala, Odisha, Punjab, Sikkim, Tamil Nadu, Uttar Pradesh, Uttarakhand and West Bengal.

Distribution in World: India, Bangladesh, Nepal, Sri Lanka and Vietnam.

21. Habenaria ramayyana

Ram. Chary & J. J. Wood, Kew Bull. 36: 235. 1981.

Tuberous herbs. Leaves narrowly elliptic to oblong-elliptic, margin minutely papillose. Flowers purplish white, in a terminal raceme. Dorsal sepal ovate-elliptic, sub-falcate; petals bipartite; lip 3-lobed; side lobes filiform, acute at apex; mid lobe deflexed; spur narrowly cylindrical; column short.

Flowering & Fruiting: July-September.

Distribution in Telangana: Nagarkurnool.

Distribution in India: Telangana.

Distribution in World: India.

22. Habenaria roxburghii

Nicolson, C. J. Saldanha & D. H. Nicolson, Fl. Hassan Distr.: 834. 1976.

Terrestrial orchid, up to 40 cm high, features 1-2 ovoid tubers. Leaves 2-6 in a rosette, flat on the ground, fleshy, sessile, broadly elliptic or orbicular, apex acute. Inflorescence a dense, cylindrical spike of fragrant, white flowers, each about 1.5 cm across. Flowers white, fragrant. Sepals broadly oblong. Petals linear, lip side lobes broad, mid lobes narrower, spur about 1.5 cm long, slender, clavate at tip, longer than the ovary; anther cells divergent; stigmatic processes sub-globose, rostellum short, triangular. Capsules oblong, 2.5 cm long.

Flowering & Fruiting: July-October.

Distribution in Telangana: Adilabad, Nizamabad, Medak, Vikarabad, Warangal and Khammam.

Distribution in India: Telangana, Andhra Pradesh, Chhattisgarh, Jharkhand, Karnataka, Kerala, Madhya Pradesh, Maharashtra, Odisha and Tamil Nadu.

Distribution in World: India and Sri Lanka.

23. Habenaria thailandica

Seidenf. (=*Habenaria gibsonii var. foetida* Blatt. & Mc Cann, J. Bombay Nat. Hist. Soc. 36: 16 1932.)

Terrestrial, perennial herb, features ellipsoid tubers. Leaves elliptic or ovate-lanceolate, 5-7 x 3-4.5 cm, transition into floral bracts. Inflorescence 10-20 cm long raceme bears 8-10 greenish-white, foul-smelling flowers. Bracts ovate-lanceolate. Sepals unequal: the dorsal sepal concave and green, while lateral sepals white. Petals bipartite. Lip tripartite, s whitish-green. Rostellum shorter than the column. Pollinia, small green appendages, curved, subsessile, beaked. Ovary is curved and beaked. Capsule fusiform.

Flowering & Fruiting: July-September.

Distribution in Telangana: Vikarabad.

Distribution in India: Telangana, Chhattisgarh, Gujarat, Karnataka, Madhya Pradesh, Maharashtra and Odisha.

Distribution in World: India, Nepal, China, Cambodia, Laos, Myanmar, Thailand and Vietnam.

24. Liparis deflexa

Hook. f. , Fl. Brit. India 5: 697. 1890.

Terrestrial herb, up to 60 cm high; pseudobulbs ovoid or oblong. Leaves 2-5, lying flat on the ground, sessile, alternate, unequal, sub-opposite, plicate, ovate or elliptic-lanceolate, entire, acuminate. Inflorescence raceme laxly many-flowered, erect, slender, glabrous, striated, winged. Floral bracts lanceolate, acuminate, deflexed. Flowers pale yellowish-green, with brownish tinge. Lip spreading, shortly clawed, flabellifom or sub-orbicular, denticulate, apex broad and emarginated. Column yellowish-white, winged, oblong. Stigma oblong-ovate. Pollinia 4, pyriform-oval. Capsules obovoid 2.5 cm long.

Flowering & Fruiting: July-August.

Distribution in Telangana: Nagarkurnool.

Distribution in India: Telangana, Andhra Pradesh, Assam, Chhattisgarh, Goa, Karnataka, Kerala, Odisha, Sikkim, Tamil Nadu, Uttarakhand and West Bengal

Distribution in World: India, Indo-China Cambodia, Laos, Myanmar, Nepal and Vietnam

25. Luisia zeylanica

Lindl., Fol. Orchid. Luisia: 3. 1853.

 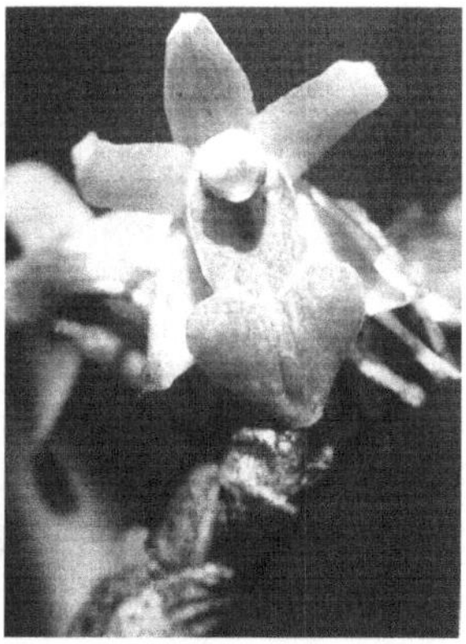

Epiphytic herbs, up to 25 cm high. Leaves alternate, green or mottled with purple, terete, apex rounded or acute. Inflorescence extra-axillary and short (around 1 cm), bears a densely flowered raceme, 1-5-flowered. Flowers greenish pink or purple, 6-8 mm across. Lip, fleshy and yellowish-maroon or dark maroon, exhibits a concave, sub-quadrate hypochile and a deflexed, cordate-ovate or cordate-triangular epichile, separated by a narrow furrow. Column maroon-yellow, oblong, with oblong-orbicular stigma. Pollinia 2, sub-globose. Capsule fusiform, 4 cm long.

Flowering & Fruiting: August-November.

Distribution in Telangana: Mahabubnagar.

Distribution in India: Telangana, Andhra Pradesh, Andaman & Nicobar Islands, Arunachal Pradesh, Assam, Bihar, Goa, Himachal Pradesh, Jharkhand, Karnataka Kerala, Madhya Pradesh, Maharashtra, Manipur, Meghalaya, Nagaland, Odisha, Sikkim, Tami Nadu, Uttarakhand and West Bengal

Distribution in World: India, Bangladesh, Bhutan, Indonesia, Myanmar, Nepal, Sri Lanka and Thailand.

26. Nervilia concolor

(Blume) Schltr., Bot. Jahrb. Syst. 45: 404. 1911. (=*Nervilia aragoana* Comm, ex Gaudich in Freyc., Voy. Bot. 422. t. 35. 1837)

Terrestrial herb, tuber globose. Leaf solitary, petiole and lamina glabrous, broadly flabellate-cordate, abruptly apiculate at tip, margin undulate. Scape flowered. Flowers green with purple veins, pendulous. Bracts deflexed, linear-lanceolate, acute, 3-nerved. Sepals subequal linear, acute, 3-nerved, petals linear, narrowly obtuse 3-nerved. Lip ovate, trilobed near the middle, white tinged with yellow veined with purple, side-lobes erect, embracing the column, obtuse, mid-lobe ovate, obtuse, entire to undulate at margins, densely pubescent along the nerves on the upper side.

Flowering & Fruiting: June-December.

Distribution in Telangana: Karimnagar and Khammam.

Distribution in India: Telangana, Andaman and Nicobar Islands, Andhra Pradesh, Assam, Bihar, Chhattisgarh, Goa, Himachal Pradesh, Jharkhand, Karnataka, Kerala, Madhya Pradesh, Maharashtra, Manipur, Meghalaya, Nagaland, Odisha, Rajasthan, Sikkim, Tamil Nadu, Uttar Pradesh, Uttarakhand and West Bengal.

Distribution in World: India, Australia, Bangladesh, Bhutan, China, Indochina, Indonesia, Japan, Malaysia, Myanmar, Nepal, New Guinea, Pacific Islands, Philippines and Thailand.

27. Oberonia ensiformis

(Sm.) Lindl., Fol. Orchid. Oberonia: 4. 1859.

Epiphytic herb, pendulous, acaulescent. Leaves coriaceous, base articulate, 4 or 5, linear-ensiform, falcate acute or acuminate. Inflorescence erect, densely many flowered, shorter than leaves. Flowers brownish yellow. Sepals reflexed, ovate, acute, subequal. Petals 3, reflexed, ovate-oblong, pubescent with blackish, stiff bristles, lip 3-lobed, concave median lobe 2-lobulate. Capsules elliptic - obovoid, ribbed.

Flowering & Fruiting: March-July.

Distribution in Telangana: Khammam, Rare, on trees in shady localities in moist deciduous forests.

Distribution in India: Telangana, Andaman & Nicobar Islands, Andhra Pradesh, Arunachal Pradesh, Karnataka, Kerala, Madhya Pradesh, Maharashtra, Manipur, Meghalaya, Mizoram, Nagaland, Odisha, Sikkim, Tamil Nadu, Uttarakhand and West Bengal.

Distribution in World: India, China, Laos, Myanmar, Nepal, Thailand and Vietnam.

28. Oberonia wightiana

Lindl., Edward's Bot. Reg. 25 (Misc.): 14. 1839.

Epiphytic, acaulescent herb. Leaves linear-oblong, acute. Inflorescence terete, raceme slender, longer than the leaves. Flowers pale yellowish-green, short-pedicelled; whorled or loosely imbricate. Sepals reflexed, ovate to ovate-oblong, obtuse or acute. Petals reflexed, linear, obtuse. Lip directed forward, spreading, quadrate, 3-lobed; lateral lobes wing-like, oblong-orbicular or rounded, folded upwards; midlobe 2-lobed; lobules diverging, oblong or ligulate, irregularly toothed; sinus with a protuberance between; disc ovate, indistinct. Column pale yellow, sub-globose. Stigma crescent-shaped. Pollinia 4, obovoid. Capsules oblong-obovoid.

Flowering & Fruiting: June-November.

Distribution in Telangana: Khammam, Rare in moist deciduous forests.

Distribution in India: Telangana, Karnataka and Tamil Nadu.

Distribution in World: India and Sri Lanka

29. Peristylus goodyeroides

(D.Don) Lindl., Gen. Sp. Orchid. Pl. 299. 1835

Terrestrial, erect herb, up to 75 cm high, with ellipsoid tubers. Leaves 3-6, clustered at the middle of stem, ovate or elliptic-oblong, acute, base sheathing. Inflorescence terminal spike, densely many flowered, 10-16 cm long. Flowers fragrant, yellowish-green or white. Bracts ovate-lanceolate, acuminate, as long as or longer than the ovary, sepals unequal, odd one ovate-oblong, subacute, lateral ones obliquely oblong, mucronate, below the apex on the back; petals obovate-rounded, strongly nerved, lip without a claw, usually 3-fid. Pollinia clavate or pyriform. Rostellum erect, toothed. Capsules ellipsoid, 1.5 cm long.

Flowering & Fruiting: August-November.

Distribution in Telangana: Nagarkurnool.

Distribution in India: Telangana, Andhra Pradesh, Arunachal Pradesh, Assam, Bihar, Chhattisgarh, Himachal Pradesh, Jharkhand, Karnataka, Kerala, Madhya Pradesh, Meghalaya, Mizoram, Odisha, Sikkim, Tamil Nadu, Tripura, Uttarakhand and West Bengal

Distribution in World: India, Bangladesh, Bhutan, China, Indonesia, Malaysia, Myanmar, Nepal, New Guinea, Philippines, Sri Lanka and Thailand.

30. Peristylus lawii

Wight, Icon. Pl. Ind. Orient. 5: t. 1695. 1851.

Terrestrial herb, up to 45 cm high, with ellipsoid to globose tubers. Leaves clustered at the middle of the stem, sessile, elliptic to narrowly oblong, entire, acute, sheathing at base, membranous, glabrous, mid vein prominent. Inflorescence a terminal spike, lax-flowered; pale green, with single bract; floral axis 11 cm long, bracts, ovate-lanceolate, acuminate, persistent. Flowers many, small, resupinate, white. Sepals white, dorsal sepal elliptic, obtuse, forming hood with petals, lateral sepals subfalcate, obtuse, entire. Petals white, concave, adnate to dorsal sepals, ovate to obtuse, 1-veined. Lip clawed, 3- lobed, mid-lobe slightly broader and longer than laterals. Pollinia 2, pyriform. Spur scrotifom. Capsules fusiform, ribbed.

Flowering & Fruiting: July-October.

Distribution in Telangana: Mahabubabad.

Distribution in India: Telangana, Andhra Pradesh, Bihar, Gujarat, Jharkhand, Karnataka, Kerala, Madhya Pradesh, Maharashtra, Odisha, Tamil Nadu, and Uttarakhand.

Distribution in World: India, Myanmar and Nepal.

31. Vanda tessellata

(Roxb.) Hook. ex G. Don, J. C. Loudon, Hort. Brit.: 372. 1830.

Epiphytic herb, up to 90 cm long. Stem covered by leaf sheaths; aerial roots stout. Leaves several, distichous, linear- oblong, keeled, auriculate at the base, strongly channeled, thickly coriaceous. Inflorescence axillary raceme, with 3-10 flowered. Flowers yellowish-green, with blue tinge, scented. Sepals yellowish-green with bluish tessellated, petals long, spreading and tessellated. Lip sessile, fleshy, 3-lobed; laterals falcate, oblong-ovate; mid lobe panduriform, truncately bifid apex. Disc with fleshy ridges. Spur flushed with purplish-violet, laterally compressed, conical. Column white, cylindrical, foot indistinct. Stigma sub-orbicular. Pollinia 2, globular. Capsules oblong, 10 cm long.

Flowering & Fruiting: July-November.

Distribution in Telangana: Adilabad, Nizamabad, Karimnagar, Rangareddy, Nalgonda and Warangal.

Distribution in India: Telangana, Andhra Pradesh, Arunachal Pradesh?, Assam, Bihar, Chhattisgarh, Dadara & Nagar Haveli, Goa, Gujarat, Jharkhand, Karnataka, Kerala, Madhya Pradesh, Maharashtra, Nagaland, Odisha, Sikkim, Tamil Nadu, Rajasthan, Tripura, Uttarakhand, Uttar Pradesh and West Bengal

Distribution in World: India, Bangladesh, China, Myanmar, Nepal, Sri Lanka and Vietnam.

32. Vanda testacea

(Lindl.) Rchb.f., Gard. Chron., n.s., 8: 166. 1877.

Epiphytic herb, up to 30 cm long. Leaves linear- oblong, distichous, channeled, stiff or curved. Inflorescence axillary, erect, raceme laxly many-flowered. Flowers yellow with brownish-pink or white lip. Petals twisted, obovate-spathulate, rounded, 5-veined. Lip 3-lobed, laterals triangular, ccl 3 mm long, mid lobe reflexed, oblong-subpanduriform, margins crenulated, apex retuse. Spur narrow, funnel-shaped. Column short, truncate. Capsules oblong-elliptic, 2.5 cm long.

Flowering & Fruiting: April-July.

Distribution in Telangana: Adilabad and Mahabubnagar.

Distribution in India: Telangana, Andhra Pradesh, Arunachal Pradesh, Assam, Chhattisgarh, Goa, Himachal Pradesh, Jharkhand, Karnataka, Kerala, Madhya Pradesh, Maharashtra, Manipur, Mizoram, Nagaland, Odisha, Sikkim, Rajasthan, Tamil Nadu, Uttarakhand, Uttar Pradesh and West Bengal

Distribution in World: India, Bangladesh, Bhutan, Myanmar, Nepal, Sri Lanka and Thailand.

33. Zeuxine longilabris

(Lindl.) Trimen, Syst. Cat. Fl. Pl. Ceylon: 90. 1885.

Terrestrial herb, up to 30 cm high. Leaves 1-6, crowded at the base, ovate-lanceolate, acute, sometimes oblique, petiole short, sheathing at base. Inflorescence terminal raceme, laxly many flowered, glandular pubescent or pilose. Floral bracts lanceolate, acuminate, hairy outside. Flowers resupinate, sepals sub equal, greenish white or reddish-brown tinge at apex, sometimes pinkish-red to reddish-brown. Petals white with base brown, falcate, oblong or obovate-oblong, obtuse, glabrous. Lip white, 3-lobed, hypochile cymbiform. Pollinia pyriform- clavate. Capsules fusiform

Flowering & Fruiting: February-April.

Distribution in Telangana: Bhadradri Kothagudem.

Distribution in India: Telangana, Arunachal Pradesh, Assam, Bihar/Jharkhand? Karnataka, Kerala, Maharashtra, Odisha, Tamil Nadu, Tripura, West Bengal

Distribution in World: India, Bangladesh, Cambodia, Nepal, Sri Lanka and Thailand

34. Zeuxine strateumatica

(L.) Schltr., Bot. Jahrb. Syst. 45: 394. 1911.

Terrestrial herb, up to 30 cm high. Leaves erect, plicate, sessile, linear, acute, entire, grass-like. Inflorescence terminal raceme, densely many flowered rarely lax, glabrous. Floral bracts greenish-brown, ovate-lanceolate, acuminate. Flowers small, white with a yellow lip. Sepals white or greenish. Petals white. Lip yellow with base white, sessile, linguiform, minutely glandular papillose. Column white, ovate-oblong. Stigmas 2, lateral, cuneate. Rostellum divided in two vertical parallel arms. Pollinia 2, pyrifom. Capsules ovoid.

Flowering & Fruiting: December-February.

Distribution in Telangana: Adilabad.

Distribution in India: Telangana, Arunachal Pradesh, Assam, Bihar, Delhi, Gujarat, Himachal Pradesh, Jammu & Kashmir, Jharkhand, Karnataka, Kerala, Madhya Pradesh, Maharashtra, Manipur, Meghalaya, Mizoram, Nagaland, Odisha, Punjab, Rajasthan, Sikkim, Tamil Nadu, Tripura, Uttarakhand, Uttar Pradesh and West Bengal.

Distribution in World: India, Afghanistan, Bangladesh, Bhutan, Borneo, Brazil, Cambodia, China, Cuba, Indonesia, Iran, Japan, Laos, Malaysia, Mexico, Myanmar, Nepal, Newguinea, Pakistan, Philippines, Saudi Arabia, South Africa, Sri Lanka, Tajikistan, Taiwan, Thailand, United States of America, Uzbekistan and Vietnam.

Cultivated

35. Spathoglottis plicata

Blume, Bijdr. Fl. Ned. Ind.: 401. 1825.

Terrestrial pseudobulbs clothed with rigid fibres of old leaves. Leaves 3-7, long-petioled, erect-recurved. Scape lateral, stout. Flowers racemed, reddish-violet, pink or rarely white; petals are significantly wider in length than sepals. Lip T-shaped, 3-lobed. Capsules green, cylindrical.

Flowering & Fruiting: Through out the year.

Distribution: This plant is widely cultivated.

Bibliography

1. Asalla, A., Ravi, G., Veeranjaneyulu, D., & Kothareddy, P. 2023. *Zeuxine longilabris* (Orchidaceae) - An addition to the orchid flora of Telangana state, India. Nelumbo, 65(1): 160–161. https://doi.org/10.20324/nelumbo/v65/2023/172686.

2. Champion H.G. and Seth S.K. 1968. A revised survey of forest types of India. Manager of Publications, Government of India, Delhi.

3. Hooker, J.D. 1888-1890. *Flora of British India*. Vols. 5 & 6. L. Reeve & Co., Kent., London.

4. IPNI (2025). The International Plant Name Index. http://www.ipni.org.

5. Mishra S., Panda S. P. and Sahoo D. 2008. Orchids of Andhra Pradesh, India. *Bulletin of Botanical Survey of India* 50(1-4): 129-146.

6. POWO 2025. Plants of the World Online. Published on the Internet; http://www.plantsoftheworldonline.org/ Retrieved 1 February 2025.

7. Pullaiah T. 2015. *Flora of Telangana- The 29th state of India*. Vol. 3. Regency Publications, New Delhi.

8. Raju V. S., Ramesh K. and Ragan A. 2020. *Habenaria commelinifolia* (Orchidaceae: Orchidinae): A new record to Telangan State, India. *Journal of Economic and Taxonomic Botany*, 43(1-4): 60-62.

9. Reddy, C.S., C. Pattnaik, M.S.R. Murthy and K. N. Reddy. 2006. Orchids of Eastern Ghats, India. *EPTRI - ENVIS News letter* 11(4): 6-12. EPTRI, Hyderabad.

10. Reddy, C.S., C. Pattnaik, M.S.R. Murthy and K. N. Reddy. 2006. Floristic census of Orchids of Eastern Ghats, India. *Botanica* 56: 79-96.

11. Reddy, KN. and C. S. Reddy. 2016. *Flora of Telangana State, India*. Bishen Singh Mahendra Pal Singh, Dehra Dun.

12. Singh, S. K., Agrawala, D. K., Jalal, J. S., Dash, S. S., Mao, A.A. & Singh, P. 2019. *Orchids of India - a pictorial guide*. Botanical Survey of India, Kolkatta.

13. Turland, N. J., Wiersema, J. H., Barrie, F. R., Greuter, W., Hawksworth, D. L., Herendeen, P.S., Knapp, S., Kusber, W. H., Li, D. Z., Marhold, K., May, T. W., McNeill, J., Monro, A. M., Prado, J., Price, M. J. & Smith, G. F. 2018. International Code of Nomenclature for algae, fungi, and plants (Shenzhen Code) adopted by the Nineteenth International Botanical Congress Shenzhen, China July 2017. Regnum Vegetabile 159. Koeltz Botanical Books, Glashütten.

ABOUT AUTHORS

Sitaram Prasad Panda has obtained M. Phil. from Ravenshaw University, Cuttack and Ph.D. degree from Utkal University, Bhubaneswar, Odisha in Botany. Presently he is working as Scientist-D, Botanical Survey of India, Deccan Regional Centre, Hyderabad. He has been working in Plant Taxonomy, Ethnobotany and Bio-diversity Conservation since more than two decades with specialization in Mangroves and Orchids. He has published more than 110 research papers on journals of national and international repute and authored 04 books.

Yasaswinee Rout is currently working as a Junior Research Fellow at Central National Herbarium (CNH), Botanical Survey of India, Kolkata, India. She is pursuing her Ph.D. in Deen Dayal Upadhyaya University, Gorakhpur. Baripada, Odisha. She is working on Endemic Orchids of India and their threat assessment. She has published about 11 research articles in national and international journals.

Dr. Peddi Harikrishna has obtained Ph.D. in Botany from Osmania University, Hyderabad. He has 16 years of research experience in Biodiversity Conservation, Plant taxonomy and Remote Sensing & GIS applications in forestry and biodiversity. He is working as Botanist in the Botanical Survey of India, Deccan Regional Centre, Hyderabad. He has published 38 research papers in peer reviewed journals and he has co-authored 6 books.